PLAY. 48 Minutes.

Table of Contents.

ISBN: 978-0-9844545-5-6
www.everydaygeniusinstitute.com

Printed in Mexico

Welcome.

You are about to become a genius student.

Take a deep breath and relax. School is about to become easier than you ever imagined.

If you are like most students, you probably developed your study habits in elementary school based on the advice of your parents or teachers. Or maybe you just developed a study system on your own and continue to use those same strategies over and over again. But have you ever stopped to consider whether your current studying habits are actually working for you?

The truth is that most students just don't know how to study efficiently. No one ever really teaches you the right way to study. Or if they do, it's based on what they think is effective, and not what actually works. Just because you are working hard does not necessarily mean you are being effective.

What top students know is that it's not how hard you study that counts, it's how smart you study that matters most.

In the pages that follow, you will meet three students who score top grades in rigorous academic environments. Not only have these students figured out how to maximize their efficiency so they can earn Straight A+s, but they each enjoy a fun and active life outside of class.

What these students have discovered is that being an A+ student is not about studying for hours and hours every night, nor is it about being 'smarter' than everyone else. The secret to being a Straight A+ student is studying smarter. And you're about to discover how simple it is to do just that.

By watching the video and reading this Strategy Blueprint, you will not only learn how to think and study like a Genius Straight A+ student, but you will be able to sail through school like one. Once you adopt these strategies into your life, you will quickly gain the skills you need to get better grades, learn more and study less.

Recommendation: Be sure to watch the included video first. Then read this Strategy Blueprint when you are done.

Discover the simply genius strategies of 3 top students.

We deconstructed the studying habits of 3 top students. We didn't just pick any Straight A+ students. We picked students that get Straight A+s and have a life! Anyone can get good grades if they spend enough time on schoolwork. Our goal was to learn how top students get their schoolwork done efficiently, score A+s easily and have extra time outside of class to do things that excite them.

To get inside the minds of these students, we interviewed them using a sophisticated behavioral modeling process. We spent hours unpacking their thinking processes, habits and strategies. And with that information, we built a model of what they do so that you can get the same results.

When we interviewed how these top students achieve such exceptional results, we analyzed:

o   How do these students achieve success, step-by-step?
o   What strategies do these students have in common?
o   What does each student do that is particularly brilliant?

Score top grades while studying less.

Everything you see in the DVD and read in this Strategy Blueprint are the real life methods that these A+ students use to score top grades. We've taken everything we learned and organized their strategies into three key areas:

Decide how to approach school.

Create the experience you want.

Develop genius study habits.

Organize your work and maximize your time.

Ace assignments and tests.

Score top grades with genius strategies.

We will teach you step-by-step what these students do to score high while studying less so that you can bring their ways of thinking into your own life. By following these steps, you will be able to get better grades with less stress. In fact, you'll find that with the right strategies, school can be more fun and easy than you ever imagined.

Meet the Genius students.

Meet three students who score top grades and still have plenty of time to play. These aren't your typical nerdy Straight A+ students who spend all their time in the library. They are students who have figured out how to study smarter, not harder, and get the most out of their entire school experience.

Jenner Fox is an A+ student from an academically rigorous public high school. In addition to taking all of the hard AP and honors classes, Jenner started a band ("Furious George" - they recently released a CD), plays competitive soccer, teaches private guitar and soccer lessons, makes fun videos with his friends and attends concerts whenever possible. What's impressive about Jenner is his ability to focus on what matters, eliminate unimportant activities and spend time on the things he really loves.

Jenner was accepted at (and is now attending) Yale University and plays on the varsity soccer team.

Andrea Vallone is entering her senior year at the top of her class in the International Baccalaureate program at the Chinese International School in Hong Kong. Her high school is ranked as one the top 20 best high schools in the world. In a way, you could say she is one of the best students in the world. Many students crumble under the pressure of the intense workload of the IB program, but Andrea makes it look easy. What's impressive about Andrea is that she has some truly genius strategies for managing her time and really understanding the material.

In addition to scoring top marks in an incredibly challenging program, Andrea plays competitive rugby, dances, volunteers, travels, has a healthy social life and makes time for her family.

Alex Freeman is an A+ student from a well respected public high school. In addition to taking all of the hard AP and honors classes, Alex plays varsity soccer and tennis, is active in Boys State (a mock government program), volunteers for political campaigns, interns at a leading product design company and has an active social life. What's impressive about Alex is that he has some truly amazing strategies for remembering information and getting his work done efficiently.

Alex was accepted at (and is now attending) his first choice school, Georgetown University.

Meet Tim Hallbom, our genius modeler.

Tim Hallbom is a world-renowned behavioral scientist. He has mastered the process of deconstructing how geniuses are thinking.

Tim is able to get inside the minds of geniuses by asking a series of unique questions that bring out conscious and subconscious behaviors, patterns and actions. He observes eye movements, body language, speech patterns and voice tonality. He gets geniuses to slow down their thought processes so that he can understand their strategies, step-by-step. He then puts their processes into simple steps that you can apply in your own life to get the same results.

Tim worked with each of the students to uncover their studying strategies. By using his proven process, he helped the students really figure out what they are doing inside their minds that makes them successful. In this product, you will discover these genius study strategies and get some insights from Tim (we call them Genius Tips) that will help you be even more successful.

Powerful strategies that will move you to the head of the class.

Whether you are a top student who wants to create more free time, a struggling student who wants to get better grades or someone who wants to make school more fun, these strategies will help you maximize your time in school.

By watching the video and absorbing the material in this Blueprint, you too will be able to:

- Have more free time while getting A+ results
- Focus your studying to learn more in less time
- Breeze through reading assignments
- Memorize facts and figures with ease
- Retain more information in your long-term memory
- Develop good relationships with your teachers
- Make boring classes interesting
- Ace assignments, tests, essays and papers
- Streamline your studying by focusing on only those things that are important
- Enjoy school in ways you never imagined possible

Straight A+ students study smarter, not harder. They think and act in ways that get them top results. Keep reading this Blueprint to learn how you can do the same.

Decide how to approach school.
Create the experience you want.

Get top grades and have time to do the fun stuff in life.

If you are like most students, you probably haven't given much thought to what you really want to get out of school. Not having clear goals is like driving all over town without knowing your final destination. The first step to increasing your efficiency is to chart a clear path for your own school experience.

Each of our Straight A+ students has a clear approach to school. They know where they want to go and have mapped out a clear route for getting there. With a clear destination, they move toward what they want with purpose and are successful at the things they pursue.

In this section we will show you how these students are thinking that makes them successful. When you think in these same ways, you will be a lot more effective in your own life. Spending time doing the excercises in this section is the surest way to become more successful in your life.

Take charge of your school experience and get the most out of it.

In this section, you will discover how to:

Set clear goals.

Have a powerful Guiding Question.

Honor 4 personal commitments.

Create good relationships with your teachers.

Set clear goals.

There is one thing we know about geniuses: they all operate from clear goals. Clear goals result in clear actions. Each of the Straight A+ students has goals for school and goals for their future. They see school as one aspect of their life. With clear goals they are able to focus their efforts and develop smart strategies to maximize their time so they can do everything they want.

The first step to increasing your effectiveness is to get clear on your own goals.

What are your goals for school, your classes and your future?

Take a moment and think about your goals for school. Do you want to get better grades? Have more free time? Make learning fun and easy? Explore an interest that excites you?

Stop here for a moment and think about it. What are your goals? As you read through each of these next pages, be sure and take the time to write down your own goals on the worksheet in the next section. Defining your goals is the most important step to getting what you want out of life. Set your goals for school, each class and your future.

You may find it challenging to set goals in each of these areas. However, if you only do one thing in this Blueprint, do this activity! Creating the experience you want requires you to decide what you want!

We recently spoke with a woman who is getting a Masters degree. When we asked her what her goals were for getting her degree, she answered, "Well, I guess my goal is to just be able to say I got this degree." That is an example of a poor goal. It came as no surprise when she then said she doesn't really enjoy school and finds it hard to get motivated to do her homework.

As you think about your goals, take a step back and ask yourself if you have good goals that will lead to your success and happiness as a person. Be sure you think about your goals and not somebody else's goals (like your parents or society's). The best goals are ones that motivate YOU to take action.

Goals for school.

School is about learning, exploring and experiencing new things. Here are some goals the A+ students have and some examples of goals you may want to incorporate into your own life. Goals for maximizing your school experience may be to:

o   Build studying and time management skills that I can continue to use forever
o   Use my time really well and don't waste any of it
o   Learn material that will allow me to be successful in college or my chosen career path
o   Have time for things I enjoy doing outside of class, like sports or my band
o   Stay relaxed and have fun in my classes
o   Build a network of friends, teachers and fellow students that can help me now and in the future
o   Balance time I spend with my girlfriend (or boyfriend) with getting my school work done
o   Spend quality time with my friends

Goals for each class.

Your goals may vary for each class. Here are some general goals our A+ students have that apply to all of their classes. Examples of some general goals for your classes may be to:

o   Impress the teacher
o   Get an A in the class
o   Make the material relevant to my everyday life
o   Learn something interesting and retain the knowledge

Goals for your future.

What are your dreams for the future? If you could do anything, what would it be? What excites when you think about doing it? If you had $100 million dollars in the bank, how would you spend your time? If you could design your dream job, what would it be? People who are succeeding in life all have clear goals they are moving toward. Set your sights high! Examples of goals for your future may be to:

o   Get into a college that I love
o   Get a great job that I enjoy at a top company
o   Make a documentary film
o   Play in a band
o   Design the next 'hot' piece of technology
o   Travel across the United States taking pictures of weird street signs
o   Volunteer to look after orphaned chimps at a wildlife sanctuary in Africa
o   Scuba dive in Papua New Guinea
o   Design clothing with a famous designer in New York
o   Run my own business

Dream big and create goals that motivate you.

How to set clear goals, step-by-step.

When you have compelling goals that you are moving toward, you'll automatically take the right actions to achieve them. Use the worksheet in the next section to define your goals. Once you've defined your goals, use the process below to make sure each of your goals is well-formed. The 'well-formed goal setting process' below was modeled from people who are highly effective at acheiving their goals. You will achieve your goals more easily when you create well-formed goals using the method below. Everyone who does this exercise benefits greatly from it.

To create a well-formed goal, ask yourself each of these questions for each of your goals.

1.   What do you want? Ask the question: What do I want to achieve here? Once you come up with an answer, ask yourself:

     o   Is this goal stated in the positive? It is very important to state what you DO want instead of what you don't want.

     o   Is this goal stated in the present tense, as if you've already achieved it?
(e.g., "I have a 3.8 GPA" is better than "I will earn a 3.8 GPA.")

     o   Is this goal specific enough? The more specific, the better.
(e.g., I want to do well in school. vs. I am earning a 3.8 GPA or higher.)

     o   Can this goal be controlled by you? Is it totally within your control to achieve it?

2. How will you know you've achieved you're goal? What is your evidence?

    o   Act "as if" you have already achieved your goal. What will you be doing once you have achieved your goal? What is your evidence that you've achieved your goal?

    o   Define the evidence through your five senses. What exactly will you see, hear and feel when you have achieved your goal? What will other people see, hear and feel when you have achieved your goal?

3. What will achieving your goal really do for you?

    o   How is having achieved your goal of value to you? How is it important to you?

    o   Once you've achieved your goal, what will that allow you to do or have or be?

4. What is the first step to achieving your goal?

    o   Is the first step specific and achievable? What is the second step?

Important note: The more vivid you can make your goals, the more successful you will be. Our minds think in pictures. Make a clear mental picture – like a photograph of yourself having achieved your goal. Once you've made a clear picture, use all of your senses and really feel what it is like to have achieved your goal.

Goal setting worksheet.
Set goals for school.

As you think about your goals for school, ask yourself these questions to get your mental juices flowing.

o   What do you want to get out of school?
o   What is important to you to do in school? Outside of school?
o   What would excite you?

Examples of Well-Formed Goals	Examples of Ill-Formed Goals
I have good enough grades, test scores and other activities that will allow me to be considered by a top college (or company).	I want to get into Stanford (or work at Apple). *This is not a well-formed goal because you might not get in for reasons that are outside of your control.*
I am at graduation receiving my diploma ranked in the top 10% of my class.	I am a really good student. *This is not well-formed because you can't make a clear mental picture out of it. What does 'really good student' mean?*

My goals for school: Set your goals for school and then ask each of the well-formed goal questions on the previous page. (Use a separate piece of paper if necessary!)

_____

_____

_____

_____

Set goals for each class.

List each of your classes and state your goals for each one. You may find that your goals apply to all of your classes. And you may have specific goals for an individual class. Ask yourself:

o   What do you want to get out of your economics class? Or science class? Study hall?
o   What's important for you to learn in this class?
o   What would excite you to learn or do in this class?

Examples of Well-Formed Goal	Examples of Ill-Formed Goals
I complete all of the assignments for each class on time.	I do well in class. *This is not well-formed because you can't make a clear mental picture out of 'do well.'*
I take at least one concept I learn every day and find out how it's relevant in the world.	I am enrolled in interesting classes. *This is not well-formed because you can't always control what classes you get enrolled in. It also relies on the teacher to make it 'interesting,' which is outside of your control.*

My goals for each class: Set your goals for each class and then ask each of the well-formed goal questions on the previous page. (Use a separate piece of paper if necessary!)

_____

_____

_____

_____

Decide how to approach school.

Set goals for your future.
As you think about your goals for the future, ask yourself these questions. Dream big!!!

o   What do you want to do after you've finished school?
o   What do you want to do, or have or be in the future?
o   Where do you see yourself in 5 years? In 10 years? In 20 years?
o   What would excite you? What is a really big dream of yours?

Examples of Well Formed Goals	Examples of Ill-Formed Goals
I am traveling through Europe for six months with a good friend.	I want to travel. *This is not well-formed because it is not specific enough. When, where and with whom?*
I am being offered a job I enjoy at the place of my dreams.	I get a good job. *This is not well-formed because you can't make a clear mental picture out of 'good job.'*

My goals for my future: Set your goals for your future and then ask each of the well-formed goal questions on the previous page. (Use a separate piece of paper if necessary!)

_____

_____

_____

_____

_____

Have a powerful Guiding Question.

All of us have "guiding questions" that run through the back of our minds in different situations. A guiding question is like a virtual question that directs our attention. It's not something we are actually thinking consciously. But it's a question that, when we stop to pay attention to it, directs our attention in the situation. It's like a silent question that is always present in the back of our minds.

This idea of a guiding question is probably something you've never thought about before. Once you become aware of it, you'll realize you have guiding questions directing your attention in every situation. (In the DVD Tim Hallbom explains this concept in detail.)

Effective students have effective guiding questions.
Each of the Straight A+ students has really powerful guiding questions that direct their attention inside and outside the classroom. For example, in the classroom:

Andrea is always asking: "How is this relevant?"
This a great question because she can find value in everything she is learning. She assumes that everything she is learning is relevant somehow and her guiding question directs her attention to figure out how it realtes to the real world.

Alex is always asking: "How is this [what I am learning] going to help me in life?"

By asking this question, Alex feels a sense of purpose and a reason for being in school. His attention is directed to learning information in a way that will serve him in the future.

Jenner is always asking: "What's important to pay attention to and spend my time on?" With this question, Jenner focuses his time on the important things that matter and ignores the things that don't. This allows him to focus on maximizing his efficiency.

Think about your guiding question. Imagine you are sitting in one of your classes. If you were asking a question that really guided your attention in the classroom, what would it be? What are you paying attention to? What is the virtual question that is subconsciously running through the back of your mind in class?

Now think about sitting down to do your homework. What question is running through the back of your mind in this situation?

Often a little change in how you think will make a big difference in your life. On the next page we'll show you some examples of guiding questions. We'll also show you how to identify your current guiding questions and incorporate powerful new ones into your life.

Recognize poor and powerful Guiding Questions.

Examples of poor guiding questions:

Some students have unproductive guiding questions that don't serve them well. Their guiding questions may not have anything to do with school or may take their attention to places that don't serve them in the best possible way. Some examples of guiding questions that won't serve you very well are:

o   How do I please everybody here?
o   How can I get through this?
o   How do I avoid getting called on by the teacher?
o   How do I impress the other students here?
o   How much longer do I have to sit here for?
o   How can I make the teacher think I've done the work?
o   When can I check Facebook (or my phone)?

Examples of powerful guiding questions:

Coming up with powerful guiding questions will go a long way to directing your attention in ways that serve you and your goals. Try out some of these powerful guiding questions. On the next page, complete the worksheet and adopt a powerful new way of thinking.

In class:
o   What is important to spend my time on here?
o   What is important to know here?
o   How will this help me in the future?
o   How is this relevant in the real world?
o   How can I get the most out of this class?
o   How can I make this fun and interesting?

Doing homework:
o How can I work efficiently here?
o How can I easily retain this knowledge?
o How can I get this done quickly and at a high level?

During school breaks:
o How can I maximize my time here?
o What schoolwork can I squeeze in and get done here?

Studying for tests:
o What do I need to focus on here?
o What information here is most important to know for the test?
o How can I focus on what I don't know well here?
o How can I easily retain this knowledge for the test?

Taking tests:
o How can I maximize my points here?
o How can I best demonstrate what I know here?
o How can I provide an A+ answer in the time I have here?

Guiding Questions Worksheet.

How to discover and adopt new Guiding Questions, step-by-step:

Adopting powerful new guiding questions is actually quite easy. Use the worksheet on the next page to write down your current guiding questions and come up with powerful new ones that may serve you even better. Follow these steps to identify your current guiding questions and incorporate powerful new ones into your life.

1. Put yourself in each situation on the next page, such as a classroom or at home doing your homework. Imagine you are actually there in that situation. Pay attention to how you are thinking in that situation. If there were a question running through the back of your mind, what would it be? Try putting yourself in the same situation but on different days and notice if the question is the same. You want to identify your general guiding question in each type of situation. If you have trouble, just ask yourself "what is the question running through the back of my mind here?' And then notice what answer you get back.

2. Generate at least three other guiding questions for each situation you think would be even better than the one your already have. (If you like your current guiding question, then keep it!) Remember: good guiding questions often start with "How" or "What."

3. Put yourself back in each situation and try out each new guiding question. Notice how it feels when you try it out. Notice how it directs your attention. Pick your favorite one.

4. Make any adjustments to your new favorite guiding question to make it even better.

5. To adopt this new guiding question, take each situation and pretend you are watching a movie with three different scenes in it. YOU are in the movie. Watch a movie of yourself in three different situations and watch yourself asking this new guiding question. For example, imagine watching a movie of yourself in three different classroom settings and watch yourself asking this new guiding question in each class.

6. Next, imagine actually being in the situation, like sitting in the classroom, and ask yourself that new guiding question. Rehearse it like you are actually there.

7. Finally, the next time you are in the situation, consciously ask yourself your new guiding question. (Write it down so you can refer to it.) When you follow this process, you will be able to automatically incorporate the new guiding question in a day or two.

Use this worksheet to identify your current guiding questions and come up with powerful new ones. Follow the instructions on pages 24-25. Use another sheet of paper if you need more space.

Situation	Current Guiding Question	Desired Guiding Question (List 3 new possibilities.)
In the classroom.		1. 2. 3.
Doing homework.		1. 2. 3.
During school breaks.		1. 2. 3.

Situation	Current Guiding Question	Desired Guiding Question (List 3 new possibilities.)
Studying for tests.		1. 2. 3.
Taking tests.		1. 2. 3.
Others? (such as reading books, doing lab assignments, participating in activities, etc.)		1. 2. 3.

Honor 4 personal commitments.

Each of the Straight A+ students makes 4 commitments to themselves and honors them. Like brushing their teeth, these are things they simply do without question.

Always do all your homework.

Each of the Straight A+ students believes wholeheartedly that doing all of the homework is essential to getting a good grade in the class. By doing a little bit of work every day and turning in all homework assignments on time, they guarantee themselves at least a B. And with a little more effort they can move the B to an A. By completing all of the homework, they spend less time studying for tests because they already know much of the material.

Stay on top of it and don't get behind.

Each of the students stresses the importance of staying on top on their work. They simply don't let themselves get behind because the stress of being behind and trying to catch up is too great. If they miss class, don't understand a concept or get a poor grade on a test, they quickly seek help from friends or teachers to get caught up right away. By staying on top of it, they reduce their stress and maximize their learning. They also find that getting ahead in the class by doing some pre-reading or working on upcoming problem sets gives them some cushion in case they do slip behind.

Avoid cramming at all costs.

Straight A+ students know that cramming to complete assignments or study for tests is an inefficient way to go through school. Cramming not only causes stress, but puts information into short term memory, which means that it is easily forgotten after the test. And when it comes time to study for a mid-term or final, you have to restudy the same material again. To avoid cramming, each of the students spreads their studying out over time and reviews their notes consistently throughout the week, the month, and the term.

Get enough sleep and physical exercise.

Everyone says to get enough sleep and exercise. Each of the Straight A+ students makes both sleep and exercise a priority. They make sure they get to bed by 10:30pm at the latest. They each have sports they play after school. They find that getting exercise and enough sleep allows them to be at the top of their game and makes them happier and more successful in school and in life.

Set your intent to adopt and honor these same commitments. You'll be amazed at the results.

Create good relationships with your teachers.

A+ students make an effort to build good relationships with their teachers. When they have a good relationship with their teacher, they enjoy the class more and find it easier to engage in the material. Put another way, these students find it much easier to get an A when they get along with the teacher and make the effort to connect.

> *"I assume the teacher is there to help me. They want me to be successful and I assume they are teaching me something for a reason."* – Alex Freeman

Having a good relationship with your teacher:

o   Makes class and learning more fun and engaging
o   Puts the teacher on your side so she is more willing to help when you need it
o   May help you get the higher grade if your grade is borderline
o   Provides you with a motivation to do well in class

Pay attention to how you sit in class.

So how do you create a good relationship with your teacher? Well, it's easier than you might think. Straight A+ students connect with their teachers by doing a few subtle, but very important things in class. To create a positive relationship with your teacher, you will notice a huge difference if you:

o   Lean forward in your chair
o   Make eye contact
o   Smile
o   Nod
o   Sit in front if possible
o   BONUS: Participate in discussions

Not this!   **This!**

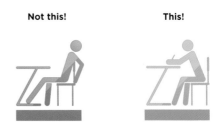

If you are in a class where the teacher doesn't like you, try leaning forward in your chair, making eye contact with your teacher, nodding and smiling. And then notice how your teacher responds. In a large study, students who did these things performed much better in class than those who didn't.

Take responsibility for your experience in class.

Chances are high you will have classes and teachers you don't like. The Straight A+ students have teachers they like and teachers they don't. The difference with these students is that they still get As in the classes they don't like.

Straight A+ students don't let bad teachers or boring classes get in their way. They take responsibility for themselves and don't blame the teacher for poor performance.

There is a simple way to overcome any class or teacher you don't like. When you find yourself in one of these situations, say to yourself: "I am absolutely responsible for my experience in this class." This puts the power back with you. Then you can find ways to make the class interesting, or at least figure out how the class works so you can get through it efficiently.

By taking responsibility for their own learning, Straight A+ students are able to score top grades in all of their classes. They don't allow any teacher or class they don't like to interfere with their goals of being successful.

> *"My backup strategy when I don't like a class is to figure out how the class works. I maximize my time in the class by focusing on what's important and getting my work done."* -Jenner Fox
>
> *"When a teacher doesn't like me, I use that as a motivation to fuel greater productivity so I can exceed their expectations."* -Andrea Vallone
>
> *"When a class or teacher is boring, I try to ask questions in the class that I think are interesting to get the discussion going in a way that is more engaging. I try to have fun with it."* -Alex Freeman

Summary of How to Approach School.

When you take the time to set goals for yourself, install powerful guiding questions, make the decision to honor the 4 personal commitments and develop good relationships with your teachers, you will be well along the path to scoring top grades and getting the most out of your school experience.

Set clear goals.   **Have a powerful Guiding Question.**   **Honor 4 personal commitments.**   **Create good relationships with your teachers.**

Develop genius study habits.
Organize your schoolwork and maximize your time.

Work hard when you work and you'll have plenty of time to enjoy other things.

Now that you've got a clear approach to school, the next step is to create powerful study habits that will allow you to get the most done in the least amount of time.

A common complaint among many students is that they don't have enough time to get through all of their work. They spend long hours and late nights and exhaust themselves trying to stay on top of it. Straight A+ students know that the problem many students have is not the available amount of hours, but rather how each hour is spent.

We heard over and over again from the Straight A+ students "Don't waste time." Getting school work done efficiently is a top goal. In order to get their work done efficiently, the students developed great strategies for organizing their time, chunking down assignments into smaller parts and using laser-like focus when they work. Straight A+ students believe that cramming and all nighters are an inefficient way to get top grades. By managing their time well, they are able to get more done in less time and enjoy other activities outside of class.

As you read this section, you will realize that being a top student has a lot to do with powerful study habits and focus. And when you adopt these habits into your life, you too will be able to score high while studying less.

In this section, you will discover how to:

Know the teacher's style.

Be a master planner.

Optimize your study location and partners.

Work in focused bursts.

Know the teacher's style.

Allow us to state the obvious: every teacher is different. What might not be so obvious is how to consciously tailor your strategy for each teacher so that you can streamline your own workload. Straight A+ students pay close attention to each teacher's style. They figure out what's important to the teacher. And then they adjust their strategy in order to give the teacher exactly what she wants and expects. By spending a bit of time analyzing each teacher's style and figuring out how the class works, you too can begin to focus your effort on what is important.

Think about each teacher you have and ask yourself these key questions so that you can better understand your teacher's style.

How does the teacher emphasize key points?
Some teachers write the really important points, formulas or keywords on the board. Others get more animated in class when they are talking about important points. Others create handouts with the important things to know. Pay close attention to how your teacher makes key points because they are the things you will likely be tested on so. Then be sure and focus your studying on those topics.

How much emphasis does the teacher place on understanding the material vs. memorizing it?
Knowing whether your teacher wants memorization of facts or a broader understanding of the themes is important. When you know what's important to the

teacher, you can focus on providing the answers the teacher is looking for on papers and tests.

How does the teacher use the reading materials? Does the teacher follow the book closely? Or does the teacher like to lecture in a more free-form way? How does the teacher expect you to use the reading material assigned? Do you need to read all of it or can you skip some of it? Do you need to take a lot of notes in class or are the key points in other handouts or materials?

How important is neatness?
If you will lose points for sloppy work, then be neat. It's silly to miss out on points for illegible work. If the teacher doesn't care, don't waste time making things tidy.

What does the teacher include on the assignments and tests?
What questions from class or the reading show up on homework assignments? What information from the homework or reading shows up on the tests? Does the teacher give out study guides?
Your goal is to figure out what type of material the teacher wants you to know. By analyzing lecture notes, homework, quizzes, tests and reading assignments, you will get a clear idea of where to spend your time studying. Ask yourself:

- o What type of information from class is on the homework?
- o What type of information from the homework is on the test?
- o What type of information from the reading is on the test?

How much partial credit can you get if you don't know an answer on an assignment or test?

Can you include some information, such as a formula or key date, and still get some credit? Some teachers give a lot of points for getting part of the answer correct, some don't give any points at all. Put your effort where it counts and only spend any time on things that get points.

How does the teacher grade?

How many points do you get for doing your homework, participating in class, taking each test, etc? How does the teacher grade assignments and tests? If the teacher will give you an A for consistently showing up and participating, then spend your time there. If you only get points on a mid-term and final, then be sure and put your effort there. If you can get points for resubmitting an assignment you received a low grade on, then re-do the work and up your grade. Or go for extra credit.

How important is class participation?

Some teachers love quiet students who actively pay attention and other teachers love outgoing students who ask lots of questions. If the teacher really values class discussion, then be sure and participate. If the teacher likes to call on students at random to answer questions from the assignments, then be sure and show up prepared.

Once you've answered these questions for each teacher, you will be well down the path of knowing what it takes to score a top grade. Use this information you've gathered to become really efficient in each class so you can focus your efforts on what is important and ignore what is not. Get good at picking out what matters and then put your attention on those things. Remember, Straight A+ students are smart about what they study. Smart studying begins in the classroom. If you aren't sure what the teacher wants or expects, be sure and simply ask the teacher!

Be a master planner.

Straight A+ students are masters at planning and scheduling their time. Each of our top students has a system to keep track of assignments and activities. Each system is a little different, yet is a system that works for them. Take these principles and develop your own rock solid system.

Keep up to the minute to-do lists and calendars. The Straight A+ students make it a top goal to complete all of the homework and stay on top of all of the material. They find the only way they can do this is to keep highly organized to-do lists and calendars. When they get an assignment, they immediately put the assignment due date on their calendar. They keep to-do lists for all assignments and spend time planning out their week so they can balance their work. They each have an organized system and stick to their schedule. Blocking out time on your calendar for sports, friends or just hanging out is just as important as scheduling your work. Schedule your free time!

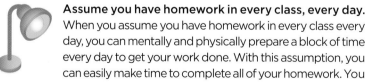

Assume you have homework in every class, every day. When you assume you have homework in every class every day, you can mentally and physically prepare a block of time every day to get your work done. With this assumption, you can easily make time to complete all of your homework. You may block out time after school, in the evening or during a period in the day where you don't have class. The key is to block out consistent chunks of time to do your work, and then follow your own schedule.

Chunk down big assignments into smaller parts.
Each of the top students is really good at chunking down large assignments into smaller activities and shorter amounts of time. For example, they take a paper they have to write and break it into different days. They research and outline the paper one day. Write it another. And edit it on a third day. Or they take a large exam and study 1 chapter a day for 3 days. By chunking large assignments into smaller parts, they avoid feeling overwhelmed. A+ students know that it is much less effective to spend 5-6 hours non-stop working on a paper or studying. It's too much for the brain to handle and it's almost impossible to focus for that long. By breaking big assignments into smaller parts, they increase their ability to learn and recall the material. They schedule these small chunks into their calendar!

Spread large assignments over time to avoid cramming.
Straight A+ students avoid cramming at all costs. Not only is cramming stressful, but it's a very inefficient way to learn. To avoid cramming, top students take large assignments and spread them over several days. They might work on a large assignment for 30 minutes each day, over a 4 day period. This strategy allows them to focus more intensely in shorter bursts and maximize long-term memory. For example, to memorize vocabulary words or a poem, they find it far more effective to do a little bit each day than try and cram it all into one sitting. If they have a light day of studying, they use the time to get ahead in another class. Or to review notes so they can keep the material fresh in their minds.

Set goals and time chunks for each study period.

Straight A+ students create a specific window of time for each assignment and set clear goals for what they will accomplish in that time period. If they are studying for a big test, they will set aside several different study sessions and focus on 1-2 chapters in each study period. If they are writing a paper, they will set a goal to accomplish a certain amount of the paper within that time frame. Set a time duration for each assignment you are working on. For example, in your schedule you might put down "Complete History Questions, 5:00-5:40pm." Clear goals focus your attention and your actions. Make it a habit to set goals for each of your study sessions.

Keep to the schedule.

Life happens and A+ students don't always keep to their schedule 100% of the time. However, they keep to their schedule 95% of the time. They sit down to do their work, even when they don't feel like it. They get themselves into a routine and stick to the routine. They find that by sticking to their own schedule, even when they aren't motivated, pays off significantly in the long run because they avoid cramming and stress.

Our A+ Student's Organizational Techniques:

Each of the A+ students has a system for staying organized. Alex has a physical and visual strategy for staying organized. He uses a colored folder for each class. Inside the colored folder on the top he puts each assignment that is currently due. (In these folders he also saves all past homework and tests.) He keeps a color coded schedule in his mind. Each block of time on his daily mental calendar represents how much homework he has in that subject. Because he assumes he has homework every night, he always has some time blocked out to get it done. Jenner uses a similar strategy of keeping a calendar in his head. Andrea, on the other hand, keeps a detailed written to-do list and calendar. She writes everything in her school planner.

It is absolutely necessary to have a reliable system that keeps you organized and on top of it. Find out what works for you and stick with it. If what you're doing isn't working, change it.

Work in focused bursts.

Do you ever notice that sometimes you are able to get a huge assignment done in 45 minutes, while other times that same assignment takes hours? Time pressure and deadlines force you to focus on getting things done. Straight A+ students know this and create self-imposed deadlines and use laser-like focus. If you are looking for the secret to how top students score high and still have free time, here it is. It's not that top students just have a special brilliance or spend countless hours studying. The truth is they do what most students don't: they focus their efforts and get things done efficiently by using a maximum amount of concentration.

By contrast, many students use an inefficient approach to studying. Many students look like they are working hard and spend lots of time in study groups and working late into the night. But due to a lack of crisp focus, self-imposed deadlines and concentration, they don't get through their work very effectively. Because these students believe they are working hard, it never occurs to them that there is a more effective way.

Straight A+ students don't fall into this rhythm of inefficient working. They know it wastes time. Instead they maximize efficiency by compressing work into short, focused sessions with clear start and end times. Once they set a time to do their work, they jam through it in that amount of time. Here is a useful formula that summarizes this point:

Work accomplished = time spent x intensity of focus*

Intensity of focus is possible only when you eliminate distractions. The students make a point of turning off their cell phone, internet/computer and TV. They eliminate external distractions, including friends, that cause them to lose focus. And they get themselves into the right mental state to get through the work. What takes most people hours to accomplish because of constant interruptions and lack of concentration, Straight A+ students get done in a fraction of the time because they maintain their intensity of focus.

Because these students compress their studying into focused bursts, they find it best to spread out their study sessions over multiple days. This gives them time between session to recharge. Lock the formula above into your memory. It's the secret to getting more done in less time.

*From Cal Newport, author of several books on succeeding in school.

How to get more done in less time, step-by-step.

Eliminate distractions.

Straight A+ students know that there is a time for work and a time for play. They make the time they spend working shorter than most people's by eliminating all distractions and jamming through their work. Many studies have come out in recent years about the inefficiency of multi-tasking. It generally takes several minutes to fully regain focus on your work after checking email or a text message. By eliminating the distractions, you will significantly improve your efficiency and quality of work. Learn to discipline yourself to eliminate distractions. You'll be amazed at the results.

Use focused bursts of energy.

Once you've eliminated distractions, you can get a lot done by using a highly focused burst of energy. Set a goal for what you want to accomplish and a time limit and then just get energized to get it done. When you give yourself a tight time limit to accomplish something, your mind automatically finds the most efficient way to get it done within that time.

Take breaks.

Your mind can only focus intensely for so long until it needs a break. Most people find that they need a 10 minute break after every hour of intense studying. This is the time to check your email, favorite websites or phone. Or just get up, walk around and grab a snack. Each of the A+ students gives themselves study breaks for 5-15 minutes, then gets back to work.

Know when you are fatigued and stop.
Your mind can only handle so much. When you find yourself re-reading the same paragraph or losing your focus, it's time to put the books down. When you are fatigued, you will retain very little information and any time spent after you've reached your limit is not going to be useful. When you are tired, you are better off stopping and then picking it back up later or in the morning when you have the energy for a focused burst of studying.

Take a moment and think about your own study habits. Do you work in a focused way or do you allow yourself to get distracted? Many students find they get distracted by Facebook, email, the internet or their phone. If you find that you are easily distracted by these things, put yourself in an environment where you don't have access to them. We spoke with one top student who removes temptation by studying in a coffee shop that doesn't have any internet access. And she leaves her phone in her car so she can't get to it. Do whatever it takes to create a space where you can maximize your focus and eliminate distractions. It's better to spend 30 really focused minutes on an assignment rather than 2 unfocused hours trying to get the same assignment done.

Genius Tip: Streamline your study habits.

We've found that all genius strategies are streamlined and efficient. What makes these study habits 'genius habits' is that they all focus on maximizing efficiency in every step of the learning process.

The students analyze everything from how the class works to what environment they study best in. They have worked out efficient time management and organizational systems that they use reliably. They have also developed really efficient strategies for learning information and recalling it later.

Most importantly, these students are able to get a lot done in a short amount of time by maximizing their focus. By working on one thing at a time with a high degree of concentration, they are able to achieve in a short time what takes many students much longer to accomplish.

IQ is a function of strategy. And when you use the right strategies, you can significantly improve your own score. By spending some time thinking about HOW to be efficient, you will find that you can make immediate and dramatic changes in your own life just by approaching the same tasks in different ways.

Spend some time analyzing where you are inefficient and model the strategies of these top students so that you can streamline your own efforts. You'll be amazed at the results.

Summary of Develop Genius Study Habits.

The study habits you've seen here are the difference between relaxed students and stressed out students. Don't fall into the trap of believing that just because you work hard that you are being effective. Dramatically increase your effectiveness by working smarter.

Know the teacher's style.

Be a master planner.

Optimize your study location and partners.

Work in focused bursts.

Ace assignments and tests.
Score top grades using these genius strategies.

Study smarter, not harder.

Having a clear approach to school and powerful study habits will go a long way toward making you a better student. You also need effective strategies for learning the material, completing the assignments and taking tests.

Most students spend more time than they need to on reading assignments, doing problem sets and writing papers. The sheer volume of work makes them feel overwhelmed and stressed out.

Here we'll show you the strategies Straight A+ students use to ace assignments and tests. When you read through each of these strategies, you'll learn how to sail through your own schoolwork.

In this section, you will learn:

Reading strategies.   **Memorization strategies.**   **Quiz/Exam studying strategy.**   **Test taking strategy.**   **Paper writing strategy.**

Reading strategies.

Think Straight A+ students do all of the assigned reading? Think again. Top students know that reading takes a lot of time and, if they've paid attention in class and taken decent notes, they can save time by reading selectively when completing assignments or studying for tests.

When you pay attention to each teacher's style, you will quickly discover what reading is important and what you can skip. Some teachers closely follow the textbook. By following along with the book in class, you can get all of your reading done in class. Other teachers don't use textbooks at all and rely on other materials. Figure out what's important to read and what's not. Pay attention to how each teacher uses the reading material, then adjust your strategy accordingly.

Most students don't take the time to figure out what is important and what is not. They spend late nights trying to read everything assigned and always feel behind. Many students often get lost in the details of the reading and try to remember every point and completely miss the big picture or big concepts. Smart students focus on the concepts!

Read textbooks selectively.
Nearly every textbook is organized by concept and the bold headlines tell you much of what you need to know. When reading a textbook, go from broad to specific. Read the bold headings first and read the small text as a last resort. The chapter

summaries are a great place to start!

Let's say your teacher gives you a homework assignments that requires you to answer questions from the reading. When you get such an assignment, read through the homework questions and answer those that you can off the top of your head based on what you remember from the lecture in class. If you can't answer the question, skim the relevant chapter and ask:

o   Does this major headline answer the question?
o   Does this sub-heading answer the question?
o   Does the paragraph heading answer the question?
o   Is there any call-out box or picture that answers this question?
o   Do I need to resort to reading the paragraph text in order to answer the question?

Read all novels and regular books if you will be tested on them. If there is a book assigned in an English or History class, and you will be tested on it, read the entire book. In these cases, the Straight A+ students assume that if they read the book, they won't need to study for any tests or quizzes. In the long run, reading the whole book saves them time because they don't have to study that material later.

Memorization strategies.

There is no getting around the fact that in school you are expected to remember a lot of material. Most students have inefficient strategies for remembering information, which causes untold amounts of anxiety on tests. Here are some great memorization strategies our Straight A+ students use.

Create relevancy.
A great way to really absorb what you are learning is to figure out how it is relevant in the world. How does what you are learning fit into the broader world? When you understand WHY something is important, you will be able to remember it much easier because you can associate it to something that you already understand. Andrea always asks the question: How is this relevant? If she can't come up with a reason on her own, she asks the teacher or her family. Or she goes online to research how it's relevant. She makes a point of connecting what she is learning to something she already knows about or something going on in the world.

Be a tourist inside the topic. Change your point of view.
One of the best ways to remember information is to create vivid mental pictures. The more of your five senses (sight, smell, sound, touch and taste) you can get involved in the picture, the easier it will be to remember things.

Alex imagines himself inside the topic he is learning about. For example, if the teacher is talking about cells in biology, he imagines he is a tourist inside the cell looking at all of the different parts. If the teacher is talking about the Roman Senate, he imagines himself as a senator in ancient Rome. He literally imagines himself being there. By creating very vivid mental pictures and experiences, it is easy for him to understand the material and recall it later.

Alex also has a great strategy for viewing information from multiple points of view. While in class, he mentally steps into his teacher's shoes and sees himself presenting the material as the teacher. By becoming the teacher during the lecture, he absorbs the information on a different level. He then imagines himself floating above the class so he can see himself and the teacher in the class. He absorbs the information from that birds-eye point of view. By shifting his point of view, he gathers information in powerful ways. Every genius we've modeled shifts their point of view to see the same thing from different angles. Try it for yourself. You'll be amazed at the new insights you gain.

Create pictures.

We know through extensive research that people remember images about 6 times better than they remember words. So if you want to improve your memory by 600%, create pictures in your mind or on paper. For example, if you are learning a foreign language, make a mental picture of each vocabulary word (like apple or car) and see that picture in your mind along with the word written on the image. Or draw pictures of concepts, formulas and timelines. Another powerful strategy is to think of images associated with what you are learning. For example, think of images that rhyme with the word or concept you need to remember. For example, Jenner uses the example of "Hippo campus is like Hippopotamus, and I'll

pretend hippopotamuses are smart" to remember a part of the **brain that deal**s with memory.

Use flashcards.

Each of the students uses flashcards as a way to **help** learn or memorize information. They each **have** different methods for creating and using the flashcards. One student likes to put pictures on the cards. Another just puts a word or two on there as a reminder for the concept he needs to remember and then he quizzes himself on that. They each use the flashcards as a way to memorize things over a period of time. Once they consistently get the answer right, they put the card away and just keep focusing on the cards with information they still need to learn. They pull out their flashcards on the bus, during a break or right before bed.

Optimize subconscious learning.

Each of the students naturally figured out what many studies have revealed: reviewing information you want to learn right before you go to bed will help you remember and recall it more easily. By reviewing things you want to remember just before you fall asleep, you are telling your subconscious mind that the information is important and you give your subconscious mind the chance to integrate the information as you sleep. To really turbocharge your learning, review that same information right when you wake up.

These students naturally discovered what many studies have revealed: we remember things better when more of our senses are engaged. When you can associate a picture, sound, smell, touch and taste to a piece of information you want to remember, you can recall the information more easily. For example, by being a tourist inside a cell you'll remember the parts of a cell better when you imagine how each part looks, feels and sounds.

Try out each of these memorization strategies. With a little practice, you will amaze yourself with your ability to learn in a whole new way. And you will find that you need to take fewer notes and study less because you naturally learn and remember the information better as you engage the right strategies (and senses) in the learning process. By using your active imagination, you will learn more effectively and efficiently. And besides, it's a much more fun way to learn!

Quiz/Exam studying strategy.

You might be surprised to learn that Straight A+ students don't study like crazy for tests the night before. By paying attention in class, doing the homework and reviewing the material over time, they have already learned much of what they need to know for the test.

To prepare for the test, each of the students figures out what will be on the test. They focus their studying on just those topics. Top students know that teachers often review the same concepts multiple times. When they prepare for exams or quizzes, the first thing they do is go back over their notes, past homework assignments and past quizzes/tests. They focus on the problems they missed or concepts they can't remember and don't waste any time studying the material they are already familiar with or studying things the teacher hasn't covered.

Get a clear idea of what will be included on the test.
Smart studying begins by getting a clear idea of what the test will include. The simplest way to find out is to simply ask your teacher. Be sure and ask what will be on the test and what won't be on the test. There is no point studying something that you won't be expected to know. Find your teacher after class or during a break and simply ask what you need to focus on. If that doesn't work, go over past notes, homework, readings and quizzes to see what types of questions show up. Spending a few minutes getting clear about what you will be tested on will save you a lot of time (and stress) when you sit down to study.

Create a study guide.
Each of the top students creates a study guide for tests. They all prefer to hand-write their study guides, saying that the act of manually writing out the study guide helps them remember the material. The study guides contain the information they don't know very well. It isn't a complete, detailed review of everything. For the topics they don't know well, they often make flashcards. They spend most of their time reviewing the topics they are least familiar with.

Study until you are able explain the concepts in your own words. As Andrea says, "I know when to stop studying when I can repeat the ideas back using my own words and I can teach what I've learned to someone else."

Passively reading and re-reading your notes is a very inefficient way to study. It's difficult to remember things this way. Instead, when you actively engage your brain in the right way, you can learn the material in a fraction of the time. To learn something efficiently, first review the concept. Then, without looking at your notes, explain the concept in your own words. Do this for every point you will be tested on. Use the memorization strategies to help you remember key points. Keep quizzing yourself until you are able to answer everything you will be tested on in your own words.

Test taking strategy.

You've studied the material and are prepared for the test. The next thing you need is a smart test taking strategy. When taking a test, your goals are to maintain a confident mental state and manage your time so you can maximize your points.

Manage your mental state.
Even if you've studied and know the material, you might do poorly on a test because you get nervous and freeze up. When you are nervous, it's difficult to recall information. There are many ways to overcome test anxiety. Alex likes to say, "Keep calm, it's JUST a piece of paper."

(In our Core Strategies of Genius product, which is available at www.everydaygeniusinstitute.com, we share many techniques for managing your mental state and improving your performance. See page 68 in this Blueprint for more information on techniques that will help you improve your mental state while taking tests.)

Read through the questions first.
Read through the questions first to get a sense of what is on the test so that you can prioritize your answers and budget your time. Your goal is to maximize points so you want to figure out how to attack the test before you start answering the first question. Also, by scanning through the test first, your mind can think about all of the questions while you are answering one of them.

Assign times to each question.

Time management is an essential part of doing well on a test. Running out of time may cause you to lose points even though you know the answers. You don't want to spend all of your time on one hard question and leave other easy questions blank. Plan out how much time you will spend on the easy, medium and hard questions. Then keep watching the clock so you can stay on track.

Do the easy ones first.

Answer the easy questions first and be sure and leave yourself enough time to get to the ones that will take you longer. This strategy will help you get on a roll and increase your confidence. It also gives your subconscious mind time to think about the harder questions. Often answering the easier questions triggers answers to the more difficult ones.

Always go for partial credit.

If you don't know the answer to a question, then absolutely put anything down so you can get partial credit! Even if all you know is the formula for a problem, or a key date or name or definition, put it down. You might not get full credit, but you will likely get some credit if you're in the ball park. If you don't know an answer, try to think of any information AROUND the topic or related to the topic. That will jog your memory. Chances are you will be able to think of SOMETHING that might result in partial credit.

Paper writing strategy.

Most students agonize over the idea of writing a paper, procrastinate and then spend hours at the last minute cramming to get it done. The whole process for many students is very stressful. There is an easier way! Each of the A+ students has a great strategy for writing winning papers without the agony most students experience.

If they have a big paper, they schedule their writing over multiple days. They spend one day reading and researching the topic and creating a clear outline for the paper. Then spend another day actually writing. If it's a long paper, they may spend a couple of days writing. The last day they spend editing their paper. By breaking the research, writing and editing into different parts, they keep their mind fresh for each part. Of course, this process may not make sense for small essays, but it is important for larger papers.

Writing requires intense concentration. Eliminating distractions while you write is the secret to producing great papers. Set clear goals for each writing session and use laser-like focus in short bursts.

Use this step-by-step strategy to write a paper:

1.   Think in shapes, sections, word counts.

Writing good papers has everything to do with planning and organization. By creating a great outline, it is easy to connect the points in your outline with words. First, get out a blank piece of paper and create a visual outline. The most important sentence in your paper is your thesis sentence – that is the sentence that answers the question your teacher asked. Get clear on your thesis statement. Then build an outline for the main points you want to cover in your paper. Wrting is much easier when you work from a clear outline.

By planning out your essay, coming up with a strong thesis and then outlining your paper in shapes, sections and word counts, you can write a winning paper in much less time than you think, without the agony!

2.   Just get it down first, then edit later.

Andrea writes a lot of papers and she says her secret is "just get anything down, let it flow however, and then come back later and edit." She says that letting the ideas flow without censoring reduces a lot of the stress of writing. Editing gives you the chance later to clean up your thoughts.

Take your outline and start writing by connecting each of the points in your outline. Remember to highlight your thesis statement in a color so you can easily refer back to it as you write. A+ essays are clearly organized and all of the sub-points support the main thesis. Make it easy on yourself and use colors to highlight your key points. And then just start writing.

3.   Go back and edit it.

It's often helpful to edit the paper a day or two after you've written it. When you come back to it, you will be mentally fresh. When you edit the paper, read it from analytical perspective. Ask yourself 'does this make sense?' Fix the parts that don't work or need to be more clear. Catch spelling and grammar mistakes.

4.   Read it from multiple points of view, especially the teacher's.

Once you've written a solid first draft, read the paper from different points of view. Imagine you are reading the paper as someone who doesn't know anything about the topic. Does it make sense? Then step into your teacher's shoes and read the paper from her perspective. Does the paper provide the information she is looking for?

Andrea literally imagines she is her teacher and adopts her teacher's way of thinking. By becoming her teacher as best as she can, she is able to be more objective about her work and notice what is or isn't working. She can see if her teacher will be pleased with what she's written.

5.   Read it out loud.

It's one thing to read your paper on your computer screen. It's a totally different experience to read it out loud. By reading your paper out loud, you will catch awkward wording, missing words, grammar errors and spelling mistakes that you often don't catch when you see words on your screen. Don't skip this step! Print out a copy of your paper, find a private spot, and read the entire paper out loud. Be sure and articulate every word. Mark any awkward wording or grammar mistakes on your printout. After you have gone through the entire paper, go back to your computer and make the changes. When you read your paper out loud, you will find that you catch many more mistakes than you will by reading and re-reading it on your computer screen.

By going over it once in this manner, you will save yourself a lot of time and turn in a much higher quality paper.

6.   Have a 3rd party check it.

The last step in writing a winning paper is to have someone like your mom, sibling, neighbor or a teacher read it. Plan enough time to have someone else read your paper because they will provide valuable feedback and catch things that you didn't. Spend time incorporating any edits. Then print it out and turn it in without looking at it again.

Genius Tip: Shift your point of view.

A well known strategy of genius is to look at something from multiple points of view. There are three points of view to consider: your own, another person's and an observer's (e.g., as a detached witness, like watching a movie of something). Geniuses like Disney, Einstein and Gandhi all actively talk about shifting their point of view and seeing things from different perspectives.

Each of the students uses this strategy of genius and actively shifts their point of view in different situations. For example, they frequently step into their teacher's shoes and see the world through their teacher's eyes. Doing this allows them to quickly understand what it takes to be successful in the class and with their assignments. It also helps them learn the material better. They also imagine they are a character in history and see the event through that point of view. You'll want to practice seeing things from different points of view! Shifting your point of view and seeing the world through another's eyes may be the most important skill you can build as a student. You can do this in your mind. You can also follow the steps below to make the experience even more vivid.

Summary of Ace Assignments and Tests.

You have learned five very powerful strategies that Straight A+ students use to ace assignments and tests. When you incorporate these strategies into your own life, you will immediately see dramatic results.

Genius Tip: Shift your point of view.

How to see things from another's point of view:
Put a card on the floor with the name of someone whose point of view you'd like to consider. For example you might put your teacher's name on the card. When you step on that card, become that person as best as you can. Hold your body like that person, move like that person and imagine that you actually are that person. While you are becoming that person as best you can:

o   Consider what matters to that person. What's important to them? What do they like and dislike?

o   Notice how that person views the world, the class, the topic, the event, other people, etc.

o   How are they thinking? Acting? Behaving? What are they seeing, hearing, feeling?

Reading strategies.

Memorization strategies.

Quiz/Exam studying strategy.

Test taking strategy.

Paper writing strategy.

Conclusion.

You just passed with flying colors!

You are on the path to becoming a genius.

Congratulations! You now know how to study smarter, score top grades and get the most out of your school experience. Once you've used these methods and experienced for yourself how easy they are, you will find you are able to enjoy school in whole new ways.

Make it a point to review this DVD and Strategy Blueprint at least once a semester so you can continue on your journey to genius.

Now go to your favorite homework spot. Sit down. Take out your books and start studying using each step in this process. You will be surprised at how much more effective you become when you practice using the strategies you've discovered here. And you'll be amazed at what you achieve.

Now go out there and do good things!

The Core Stratregies of Genius:
7 proven techniques to unlock your inner genius.

Take your genius to a whole new level.

Our Core Strategies of Genius product includes seven proven techniques that will help you unleash your inner genius. On the next three pages we provide a brief description of each technique we feature in this product. We then share some specific way you can apply each process in the product to becoming a better student. As you read through each of these strategies, you will discover powerful ways to achieve success in your life.

Order this product directly from our website at:

www.everydaygeniusinstitute.com

Core Strategies of Genius Technique	Ideas for how you can use this technique to become a better student.

WELL FORMED GOALS:
Achieve more in less time

Straight A+ students are successful because they operate from high quality goals in and outside the classroom. You will naturally become a better student by getting clear on your own goals.

The Well Formed Goal process will help you effectively set goals so that your conscious and subconscious behavior naturally support your efforts. This is a goal setting strategy modeled from people who are highly effective at setting and achieving goals. It's unlike any goal setting process you've ever seen. Using this process will get you powerful results that may even surprise you.

NEW BEHAVIOR GENERATOR:
Install a new habit easily

Learning genius processes often requires remembering to do new things. The New Behavior Generator is a way to program yourself now to remember later. Use this technique to make learning anything easier. Instantly lock in and remember information taught in lectures, steps to math or science problems, or instructions for completing homework assignments. Use it to install new study habits automatically. This is an incredibly powerful technique that will turbo-charge your effectiveness as a student.

Core Strategies of Genius Technique	Ideas for how you can use this technique to become a better student.
 PIECE OF CAKE: Make it easy to learn	Because we don't realize how simple it can be to learn something new, we often give up before we master it. Using the Piece of Cake process will make your journey to become a better student much more fun and easy. Use this technique to make writing papers feel easy. Use it to make math homework feel easy. Or use it on any part of the school that might feel challenging to you.
 EYE MOVEMENT INTEGREATION: Eliminate feelings of anxiety, frustration or fear	Although it may seem a little strange, this process will help you eliminate any feelings of frustration, fear, self-doubt or lack of confidence as you go through school. It's a great technique to help with test anxiety. It's quick and easy to do and uses your own neurology so that you can use more of your brain power to break through any limitations to your own success. You can also use this technique to help you access your best mental states, such as curiosity, so you can make learning fun.

Core Strategies of Genius Technique	Ideas for how you can use this technique to become a better student.
MENTAL MENTORS: Receive helpful advice from people you respect	Most of us have people in our lives who believe in us. They offer us useful advice, a new perspective or get us to consider something we hadn't thought of. The Mental Mentor process will give you a way to get insights that may not have occurred to you on your own. It's a way to see information from your teacher's point of view. Take advantage of expert knowledge that is a part of your own mental processing and become a better student.
CIRCLE OF EXCELLENCE: Step into powerful emotional states on demand	Creating a Circle of Excellence is a way to quickly and easily step into your most powerful mental state. This process will teach you how to do that on demand. You can build a Circle of Excellence to be at your best, most confident state when taking tests. Feel confident and excited when you need to speak in front of the class. You can also use this process to create a powerful learning state as you listen to lectures or study material outside of class. You will be amazed at the power of this technique.
MOTIVATION STRATEGY: Feel highly motivated to accomplish a task	It's amazing what we can accomplish when we feel motivated! This process will teach you how to easily motivate yourself to study and do homework, even when you don't feel like it. It will allow you to make schoolwork fun and enjoyable.

About us.

At the Everyday Genius Institute, we take people who are exceptional at what they do, deconstruct their process and then teach you exactly how you can get the same results.

In our Think Like a Genius series, we reveal for the first time exactly how geniuses are thinking and then teach you how to do the same. By modeling the strategies of the best in the world, you will unlock your inner genius, cut years off your learning curve and achieve mastery easier than you ever imagined.

To learn more about us and the strategies of genius we've deconstructed on topics ranging from wine tasting to sales, go online and visit us at **www.everydaygeniusinstitute.com.**

Additional resources you might find useful.

So much of being a student involves memorizing and remembering information. In addition to the learning and memory strategies we present here, you may it helpful to add even more tecniques to your toolkit. We scoured the earth and found one great resource that will help any student.

Chester Santos is the 2008 National Memory Champion. He teaches some very powerful memorization techniques that will help any student remember a lot of information quickly and easily. Check out his site and learn more about his methods at www.chestersantos.net.

Notes:

Notes:

Notes:

Notes:

Notes:

Notes:

everyday**genius**
INSTITUTE